**Mr Steggels
Selective Achievement Tests
Level 2**

Suitable for ages 8 – 10

Each test contains 35 mixed questions

- 15 general ability
- 10 reading comprehension
- 10 mathematics

A score summary chart is printed at the end of each test

Contents

Test 1	page 2
Test 2	page 12
Test 3	page 22
Test 4	page 32
Test 5	page 42

Solutions

Test 1	page 52
Test 2	page 53
Test 3	page 55
Test 4	page 57
Test 5	page 59

Copyright © 2017 Simon Steggels
All rights reserved

No part of this book may be reproduced, stored in a retrieval system, communicated or transmitted in any form or by any means without prior written permission. All inquiries should be made to the publisher.

ISBN 978-0-6480967-1-9

Published by
Advanced Instruction Pty Ltd
www.advancedinstruction.com.au

© MR STEGGELS ADVANCED INSTRUCTION PTY LTD

Test 1

Read the text and answer questions 1—5

Garden Fresh Restaurant Kids' menu	41 Bolt Street Westside Ph 283 4571
Snacks	$6
Wedges Crunchy wedges served with tomato sauce	Fish fingers Two fish fingers served with sauce or light mayonnaise
Meals	$12
Beef burger Lean beef patty, tomato, lettuce, cheese on a sesame seed bun	Nuggets and chips 6 free range chicken nuggets, baked not fried, served with chips and sauce
Chicken Burger Free range chicken breast fillet, tomato, lettuce, cheese on a sesame seed bun	Fish and chips 1 piece of fish, 1 potato scallop served with chips and sauce
Drinks	$2.50
Juices—orange, pineapple, blackcurrant	Soft drinks—lemonade, cola, orange, creaming soda, passion fruit
Water—bottled spring water	Frozen ice drinks—cola, lemonade, bubblegum, berry, cherry
Desserts	$8
Nutella Pizza A light pizza base topped with a thick coating of Nutella and served with ice cream	Banana split Banana, ice cream, sprinkles and your choice of chocolate, strawberry or caramel sauce
Specials	Opening hours
Kids eat free* Tuesday from 5pm – 7pm * Two adult meals must be ordered	Monday to Friday 11am to 9pm Saturday 11am to 10pm Sunday closed

1. This text can best be described as

    A   a restaurant
    B   a menu
    C   a story
    D   an explanation

2. The main purpose of this text is to

    A   give information
    B   get the reader to buy something
    C   explain what Garden Fresh means
    D   retell a series of events

3. Which is true?

    A   Garden Fresh restaurant is not open on Sundays
    B   Kids can eat free but their parents must buy food
    C   There are two desserts on the menu
    D   all of the above

4. Which soft drink is not listed on the menu?

    A   cola
    B   creaming soda
    C   lemon
    D   passion fruit

5. I ordered a beef burger, a frozen ice cola and a banana split. How much did I spend?

    A $20.00
    B $20.50
    C $22.50
    D $16.50

6. Which letters are missing in this series?

   A   D   G   __   M

   A   H
   B   I
   C   J
   D   K

7. One jug has 120mL of water A second jug has 220mL of water. How much water should I pour from the second jug into the first so that both jugs have the same amount of water?

   A   80mL
   B   700mL
   C   100mL
   D   50mL

8. In a certain code, the words **bet**, **tim** and **bit** are written 452, 251 and 432, but not necessarily in that order. How would **emit** be written using this code?

   A   2531
   B   3154
   C   3152
   D   2513

9. There are 25 students in the hall. Twelve girls leave to go to choir practice. Nine boys arrive with their teacher. How many people are in the hall now?

   A   47
   B   38
   C   23
   D   22

10. An **illustrator**

    A   teaches
    B   writes
    C   draws
    D   speaks

© MR STEGGELS ADVANCED INSTRUCTION PTY LTD

11. Which is the odd one out?

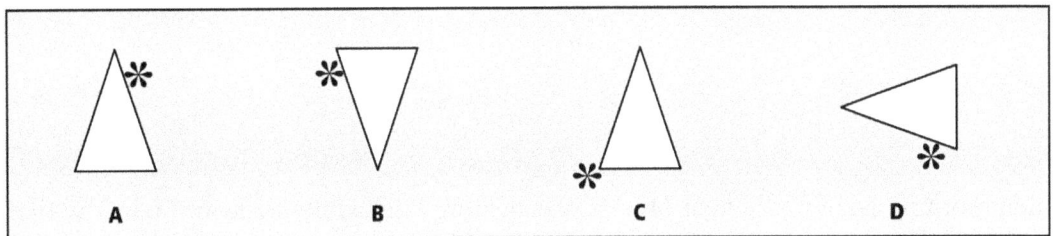

12. Which is the odd one out?

    A   cenitmetre
    B   metre
    C   kilometre
    D   milllitre

13. I am thinking of three numbers. They are next to each other, like 1, 2 and 3. These three numbers add up to 36. The smallest of these numbers is

    A   10
    B   11
    C   12
    D   13

14. Three bananas weigh the same as one rock melon. Three rock melon weigh the same as one watermelon. How many bananas weigh the same as one watermelon?

    A   6
    B   9
    C   12
    D   15

15. Which word can be placed before these words to make new, compound words?

    _____one   _____thing   _____times   _____how

    A   any
    B   no
    C   good
    D   some

© MR STEGGELS ADVANCED INSTRUCTION PTY LTD

Read the text and answer questions 16—20

Wash out

I woke up this morning and I could hear rain. It was beating against my bedroom window like my baby brother beating on his drum.

It had been raining all week. Our class had been stuck inside at recess and lunch every day. School seemed to drag on forever. I couldn't wait for the weekend.

Some people like being inside when it's raining. They love cuddling up in bed with a book, under the covers. They might peak outside every now and then, happy that they're warm and dry.

Not me.

I like being outside. In any weather. Especially because my favourite game is played outside. I like playing soccer rain, hail or shine. But this week's game was going to be a washout. The council had already closed the local soccer field because it was underwater.

None of my friends would be able to come over in this weather. So, it looks like I'll have to play with my little brother all day. He's a real pain if he doesn't get his own way—like most two years olds. And, of course, Mum and Dad always **side with** him.

Maybe I'll just stay in bed and pretend to be sick. On second thoughts, if I do that, I won't be able to play on my computer. Mum won't let me. Even if I'm home all day from school with the flu, I have to stay in bed and rest!

Well, I suppose I'd better get up and make the best of it.

© MR STEGGELS ADVANCED INSTRUCTION PTY LTD

16. We can tell that the writer is

    A   happy
    B   sad
    C   bored
    D   content

17. It is a **fact**, not an **opinion** that

    A   the writer's little brother is a pain if he doesn't get his own way
    B   the council closed the soccer field because it was underwater
    C   school seemed to drag on forever
    D   some people like the rain

18. The phrase **side with** can best be replaced by

    A   play
    B   protect
    C   fight
    D   agree

19. The writer is unlike other kids because he

    A   enjoys soccer
    B   does not like playing with his little brother
    C   loves cuddling up in bed with a book
    D   doesn't mind being outside in any type of weather

20. Which is true?

    A   The writer's baby brother woke him up with his drum playing
    B   It had been raining all weekend
    C   The author is happy that he is warm and dry inside
    D   Students had been kept inside at break times during the week

© MR STEGGELS ADVANCED INSTRUCTION PTY LTD

21. Someone who **works with wood** is called a

    A   deckhand
    B   shearer
    C   carpenter
    D   woodsman

22. Find the rule connecting the numbers in the first row with those in the second row. Which number completes the pattern?

1st	3	6	9	11
2nd	9	36	81	?

    A   22
    B   110
    C   123
    D   121

23. I tossed two six-sided dice. How many different combinations of numbers could I get?

    A   6
    B   12
    C   21
    D   36

24. Which is the odd one out?

    A   hornet
    B   locust
    C   husky
    D   fly

25. How many squares of any size are in this shape?

    A   8
    B   10
    C   11
    D   12

26. **Melon** is to **fruit** as **parsley** is to

   A   vegetable
   B   herb
   C   flower
   D   fruit

27. In a long jump competition, Sam jumped 2.98 m. Harvey jumped 6 cm further than Sam. Yuri jumped 7cm further than Harvey. How far did Yuri jump?

   A   3.01m
   B   3.10m
   C   3.11m
   D   3.12m

28. Rearrange these words into a coherent sentence

   their   approaching   saw   the   bus   stop   they

   If the first word of this sentence is **they**, what would be the last word?

   A   approaching
   B   stop
   C   bus
   D   saw

29. In a certain code, **new** is written 391 and **erase** is written 97589. How would **answer** be written using this code?

   A   538179
   B   583197
   C   538917
   D   538197

© MR STEGGELS ADVANCED INSTRUCTION PTY LTD

30. This chart shows when students get to school. How many students get to school before 9am?

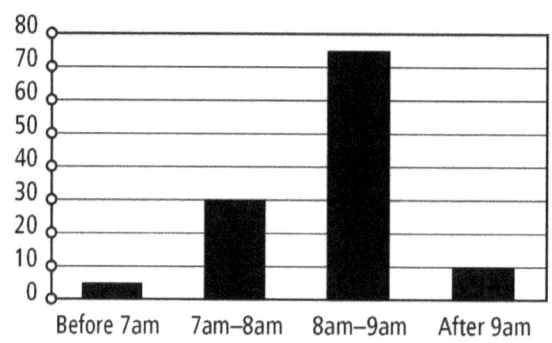

    A   35
    B   105
    C   110
    D   120

31. Unscramble these words to find the only one that is **not a colour**

    A   obnrw
    B   dogl
    C   ganoer
    D   preap

32. Which shape is next in the pattern?

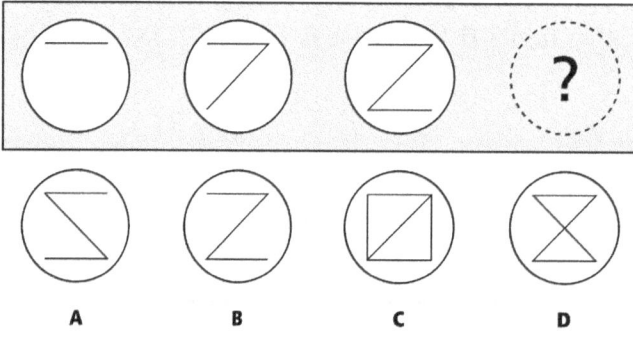

33. One shirt and one pair of shorts cost $20. One shirt and two pairs of shorts cost $32. How much does one shirt cost?

    A $8
    B $12
    C $24
    D $52

© MR STEGGELS ADVANCED INSTRUCTION PTY LTD

34. Solve this visual puzzle

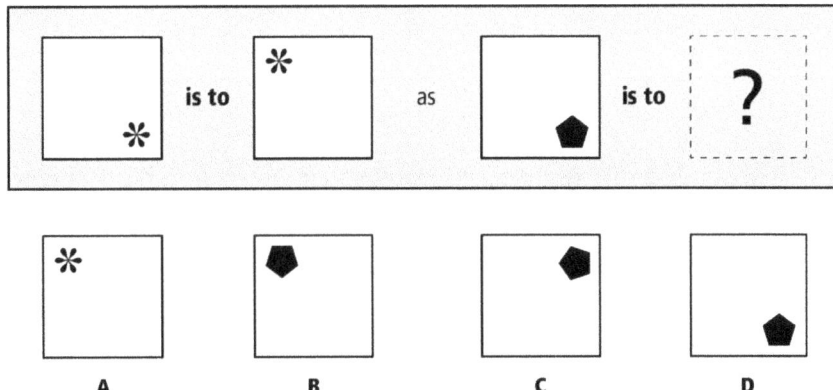

35. In a certain code, the letter a = z, b = y, c = x and so on.

In the same code, l =

A   n
B   m
C   o
D   p

© MR STEGGELS ADVANCED INSTRUCTION PTY LTD

END OF TEST

Test 2

Read the text and answer questions 1—5

    I had a dream. Well, it was more of a nightmare. I was at sea in the middle of a storm. My boat was a bathtub.

    The water was dark. Inky black. The waves were enormous. They kept crashing on me, filling the tub with water. I only had a soup spoon to empty the tub. Water was coming in faster than I could spoon it out. I was expecting to sink any minute.

    Then, lightning started, followed by thunder. Sparks of white light flashed across the sky. They lit up the heavy, dark clouds. They jumped from cloud to cloud like crazy monkeys swinging through the jungle. The thunder sounded like an angry giant roaring above the clouds. The wind was like a hurricane. The rain hit my head and shoulders hard. I wasn't even wearing a raincoat. Just my shower cap.

    I saw a huge wave coming toward me. It was taller than a building. It almost blocked out the clouds. It was curling over at the top. There was no way to get over it. I closed my eyes. Just when I thought I was going disappear forever, I woke up.

    How did I survive that huge storm at sea, floating over giant waves in only a bathtub? Dreams can be very strange. I must remember not to fall asleep in the bathtub …

© MR STEGGELS ADVANCED INSTRUCTION PTY LTD

1. What was not part of the writer's dream?

    A   a bathtub
    B   shower cap
    C   umbrella
    D   soup spoon

2. What happens third?

    A   Lightning started
    B   I saw a huge wave coming toward me
    C   I woke up
    D   Water was coming in faster than I could spoon it out

3. The writer compares the thunder to

    A   a hurricane
    B   crazy monkeys swinging from tree to tree
    C   an angry giant
    D   sparks of white light

4. Which word means **very large in size**?

    A   giant
    B   huge
    C   enormous
    D   all of the above

5. What is the most suitable title for this text?

    A   How to survive a storm at sea
    B   What causes lightning and thunder?
    C   Nightmare at sea
    D   Bath time

© MR STEGGELS ADVANCED INSTRUCTION PTY LTD

6. Choose the category to which the other words belong

   A   flour
   B   ingredients
   C   eggs
   D   sugar

7. **Daisy** is to **flower** as _____ is to _____

   A   drill   tool
   B   flower   flour
   C   car   road
   D   nail   wood

8. Complete the following saying

   _____ is man's best friend.

   A   Money
   B   A dog
   C   A friend
   D   Company

9. I am thinking of 2 numbers. They add together to make 27. One number is double the other. The difference between these two numbers is

   A   7
   B   8
   C   9
   D   10

10. Milly is not as old as Betty. Joan is younger than Betty. Joan is older than Milly. When listed from youngest to oldest, the order is

    A   Betty, Millly, Joan
    B   Betty, Joan, Milly
    C   Joan, Milly, Betty
    D   Milly, Joan, Betty

© MR STEGGELS ADVANCED INSTRUCTION PTY LTD

Use this calendar to answer questions 11—12

S	M	T	W	T	F	S
		1	2	3	4	5
6	7	8	9	10	11	12
13	14	15	16	17	18	19
20	21	22	23	24	25	26
27	28	29	30	31		

11. Which is false?

    A   There are four weekends in this month
    B   They are more odd numbered days than even numbered days
    C   There are four full weeks in this month
    D   There are five Tuesdays in this month

12. The month shown on the calendar could not be

    A   January
    B   November
    C   July
    D   October

13. Rearrange all of the words to make a coherent sentence

    rules   the   road   must   follow   every   driver

    The last word in the new sentence is

    A   driver
    B   follow
    C   rules
    D   road

14. These number patterns follow the same rule. What number completes the third set?

    3, 9, 4   4, 12, 7   6, 18, ___

    A   10
    B   12
    C   13
    D   14

© MR STEGGELS ADVANCED INSTRUCTION PTY LTD

15. The word **danger** is most opposite in meaning to

    A   threat
    B   safety
    C   stranger
    D   accident

16. What number is missing from this number sentence?

    $$6 \times \underline{} = 36 \times 2$$

    A   14
    B   13
    C   12
    D   6

17. **Soap** is to **clean** as **desk** is to

    A   classroom
    B   office
    C   writing
    D   wood

18. If the black section of this shape is worth 2, what is the whole shape worth?

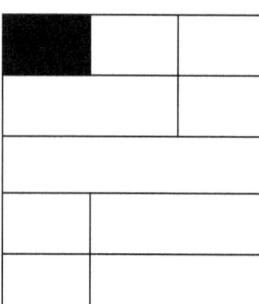

    A   15
    B   18
    C   30
    D   36

© MR STEGGELS ADVANCED INSTRUCTION PTY LTD

19. I was riding my bike along the coast when I came across this sign. How far apart are Sandy beach and Shark bay?

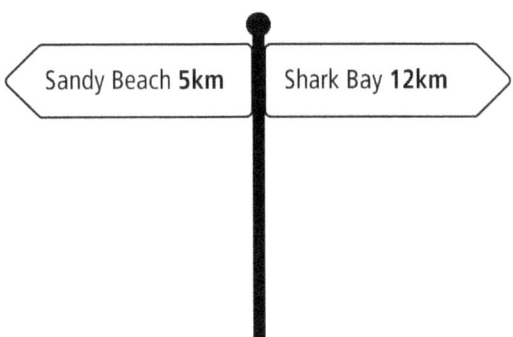

- A   7 km
- B   8 km
- C   17 km
- D   22 km

20. Which shape completes the larger pattern?

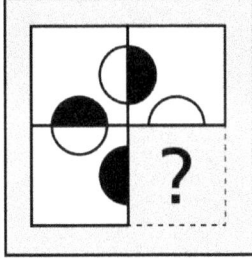 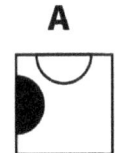 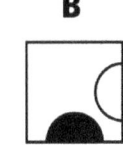 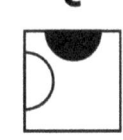 

21. If **sort** + **tame** = **some** then **seal** + **chat** =

- A   seal
- B   alat
- C   seat
- D   hats

22. Which word can be used to end the first word and begin the second?

sea_____ / _____line

- A   fish
- B   clothes
- C   side
- D   ocean

23. Which code matches the shape at the end of the line?

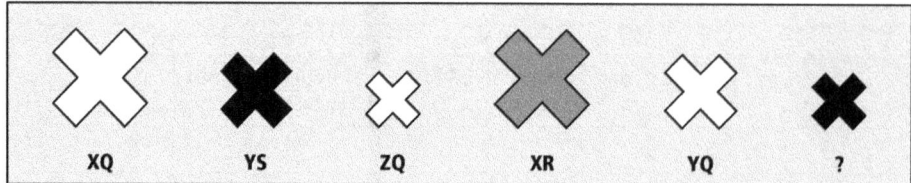

- A XS
- B ZS
- C YQ
- D ZR

24. Use the numbers 2, 3, 6, 7, 9, and 10 to make the sum of each row and column equal to 18. Which number should replace the question mark?

5	4	
		?
	8	

- A 9
- B 7
- C 6
- D 2

25. Which pattern is a reflection of the shape on the left?

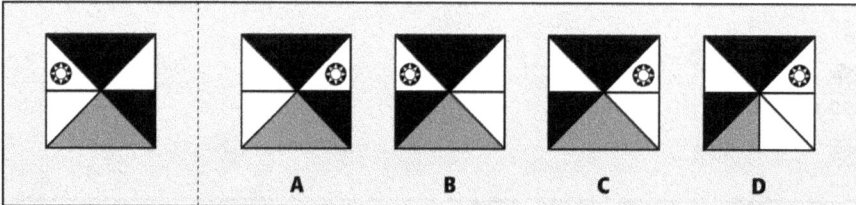

26. Which word has the same meaning as **entire**?

- A long
- B tired
- C most
- D complete

27. Which word belongs in this group of similar words?

    Adelaide   Sydney   Melbourne   Alice Springs

    A   Brisbane
    B   Queensland
    C   Australia
    D   Gold Coast

28. Which word is made from the same letters as **learnt**?

    A   neater
    B   taller
    C   antler
    D   central

29. Which number comes next?

    54, 48, 42, 36, 30, ___

    A   26
    B   25
    C   24
    D   20

30. A **son** always has a

    A   daughter
    B   sister
    C   mother
    D   uncle

© MR STEGGELS ADVANCED INSTRUCTION PTY LTD

Read the text and answer questions 31—35

Home made pizza

You will need an adult to help because pizza is cooked in a very hot oven, and some ingredients need to be cut with a knife. You will need to use an oven tray and oven mitt, so you don't burn yourself.

Ingredients

    pizza base (you can buy pizza bases from your local supermarket)
    olive oil
    tomato paste (or tomato sauce)
    grated cheese (mozzarella and tasty)
    various toppings (sliced onions, chopped capsicum, minced meat, sausage, pineapple chunks, sliced mushrooms, sliced olives and chopped herbs)

Method

1. Set the oven to 250 °C (very hot)
2. Wipe olive oil over tray
3. Put pizza base on tray
4. Spread tomato paste evenly over base
5. Arrange toppings on tomato paste
6. Sprinkle grated cheese on top
7. Put tray in oven using oven mitt
8. Cook for 10 minutes or until cheese melts and base edges turn brown
9. Remove carefully using oven mitt
10. Slice and serve

Enjoy your delicious home made pizza!

31. This text is aimed at

    A   adults who want to cook with their kids
    B   readers who want to be entertained
    C   adults only
    D   kids who want to make home made pizza

32. Which two words share the same meaning?

    A   slice, serve
    B   base, pizza
    C   toppings, ingredients
    D   sliced, grated

33. Which step comes first?

    A   sprinkle on grated cheese
    B   spread tomato paste evenly on base
    C   arrange toppings
    D   cook for 10 minutes

34. An adult helper is needed

    A   because the recipe is very difficult
    B   because kids don't usually like making pizza
    C   to read the recipe
    D   because there is a chance of getting hurt while making this recipe

35. We can conclude that

    A   not all of the toppings need to be used—the reader can choose which ones they like
    B   all of the toppings that are listed must be included on the pizza
    C   the pizza base must be bought from the local supermarket
    D   the reader has never made pizza before

© MR STEGGELS ADVANCED INSTRUCTION PTY LTD

END OF TEST

Test 3

1. I have four playing cards—Ace, King, Queen & Jack. The Queen is to the left of the Ace. The Jack is to the right of the Ace. The King is furthest from the Queen. What is the order of the cards from left to right?

    A   Ace, King, Queen, Jack
    B   Queen, Ace, Jack, King
    C   King, Ace, Jack, Queen
    D   Queen, Jack, Ace, King

2. **Garden** is to **flowers** as _____ to _____.

    A   book   pages
    B   painting   drawing
    C   sink   water
    D   sock   pair

3. I am thinking of two words that sound the same but are spelt differently and that have these two meanings

    (1) found and stopped a person trying to escape
    (2) an area drawn on the ground that is used for playing sport

    These words begin with the letter

    A   f
    B   g
    C   c
    D   a

4. In a certain code, **cater** is written   % # @ ! >

    How would the word **react** be written in the same code?

    A   > # ! % @
    B   > ! # % @
    C   > ! # @ %
    D   ! @ % > #

© MR STEGGELS ADVANCED INSTRUCTION PTY LTD

5. I went to the shop with a $10 note. I spent $1.50 on a pen and $2.30 on a pad. How much change should I get?

    A $3.80
    B $6.20
    C $6.80
    D $7.20

6. The word most similar to **useful** is

    A   handy
    B   expert
    C   neat
    D   useless

7. Which shape has two faces that are triangles?

    A   triangular pyramid
    B   square pyramid
    C   triangular prism
    D   cube

8. What number is missing from this pattern?

    2, 8, 6, 12, 10, 16, ___, 20

    A   19
    B   18
    C   14
    D   12

9. A **car** always has

    A   passengers
    B   four doors
    C   a roof
    D   wheels

© MR STEGGELS ADVANCED INSTRUCTION PTY LTD

Read the following passage and answer questions 10—14

New house

We just moved into a new house. Everyone in my family loves it, but I don't.

It's bigger than our old house. The bedrooms are bigger. The kitchen is big. The living room is big. There are three bathrooms. There is even a play area just for my sister and me. But something just doesn't feel _____(10).

It's not the dark basement beneath the house or the lonely room at the top of the stairs. There are no ghosts. Well, not that I know of. I just get the feeling I have lived in this house before. But I _____ (11) have. I have only lived in one house—the one we just moved from.

Even before we went inside to see our new house, I knew where _____ (12) was. I showed my mother the door to the laundry—it's hidden in a wall in the kitchen. And I showed my sister how to get into the play area from the passageway in our bedrooms. The lady who showed us the house was confused. Even she didn't know about the _____ (13).

After we moved in, I tried to forget my worries and start a new life in a new house. And then one day, my sister and I crept up to the room at the top of the stairs. It was empty except for a few pictures on the walls that the previous owners had not taken with them.

My sister looked at each one closely. Then she gasped. She turned to me with a strange look on her face. I went over and saw an old black and white photo. A girl my age was standing in front of the house. There was writing in black pen at the bottom. It said, Ellie, 1965.

The girl in the photograph was_____ (14).

© MR STEGGELS ADVANCED INSTRUCTION PTY LTD

10. Choose the most suitable word for position 10

   A   big
   B   right
   C   different
   D   happy

11. Choose the most suitable word for position 11

   A   shouldn't
   B   must
   C   couldn't
   D   should

12. Choose the most suitable word for position 12

   A   everything
   B   the kitchen
   C   it
   D   things

13. Choose the most suitable word(s) for position 13

   A   bedrooms
   B   feeling I had
   C   house
   D   passageway

14. Choose the most suitable word(s) for position 14

   A   my sister
   B   me
   C   alive
   D   smiling

© MR STEGGELS ADVANCED INSTRUCTION PTY LTD

15. I bought 2 apples for $4.10. How much would 3 apples cost?

    A $ 6.30
    B $ 6.20
    C $ 6.15
    D $ 5.15

16. Which number completes the pattern?

X	3	4	6	8	9
Y	11	15	23	31	?

    A   39
    B   40
    C   37
    D   35

17. Which shape completes the second pair in the same way as the first?

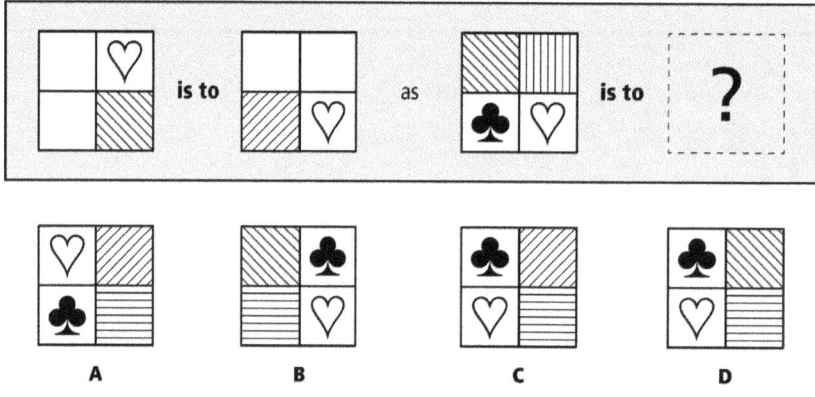

18. What should you do with a **beverage**?

    A   put your clothes in it
    B   wear it on your shirt
    C   drink it
    D   keep it as a pet

© MR STEGGELS ADVANCED INSTRUCTION PTY LTD

19. Choose two words, one from each group, to make a new word.

Group A	foot	moon	some	him
Group B	light	selves	her	wait

The new word beings with

A   m
B   f
C   s
D   h

20. In a certain code, the words **hem**, **him** and **mit** are written **634**, **256** and **236** but not necessarily in that order. How would the word **time** be written in the same code?

A   4356
B   4365
C   6543
D   4352

21. Which letter will end the first word and start the second word?

gan __ / __ ong

A   t
B   k
C   s
D   g

22. What fraction of the shape is shaded?

A   one quarter
B   one third
C   one half
D   three quarters

23. Liam is one year older than Ben. Ben is two years older than Ryan. Frank is 12 and is twice as old as Ryan. How old is Liam?

    A   10
    B   9
    C   8
    D   7

24. In a certain code, the word **hero** is written **jgtq**

In the same code, how would the word **fowl** be written?

    A   hqyn
    B   dmuj
    C   hpxn
    D   hqxn

25. Which tile should replace the missing square?

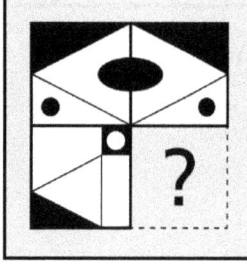   A 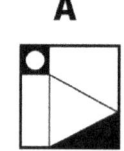   B 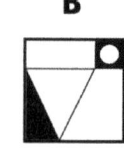   C 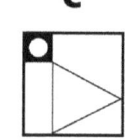   D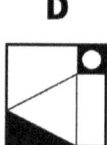

26. The saying **as thick as thieves** means

    A   thieves are very thick
    B   very close friends
    C   thieves always trust each other
    D   you can't trust anyone

© MR STEGGELS ADVANCED INSTRUCTION PTY LTD

27. Which statement about the spinner is true?

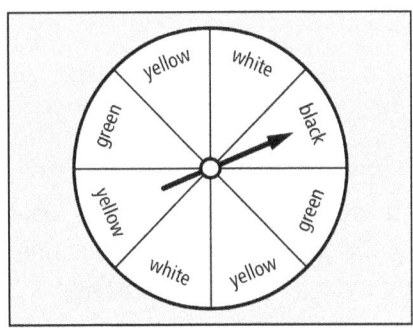

- A   There is more chance of spinning black than white
- B   The spinner will land on green more than any other colour
- C   There is more chance of spinning green than yellow
- D   There is an equal chance of spinning green or white

28. Two days ago it was Sunday. What day of the week will it be ten days from today?

- A   Friday
- B   Saturday
- C   Thursday
- D   Tuesday

29. Which is the odd one out?

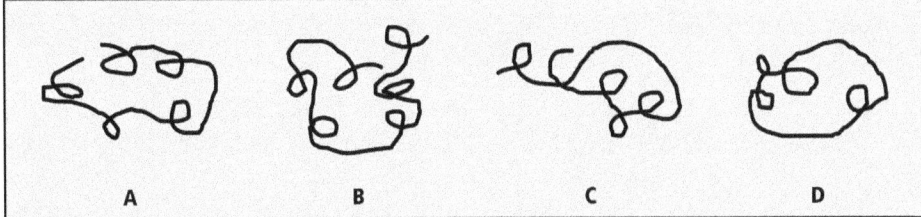

30. Choose the most suitable words to complete the sentence

In winter, the (cold / weather / temperature) is (lower / fine / comfortable) so people mainly stay (outdoors / indoors / together).

A	cold	lower	indoors
B	temperature	lower	together
C	temperature	lower	indoors
D	weather	fine	indoors

Read the text and answer questions 31—35

The human brain

Your brain controls your body. It allows you to move, to learn, to remember, to feel, to dream and to solve problems. It sends signals to your eyes, your ears, your nose, your fingertips, your heart. It is like a super fast computer. It keeps working even when you are asleep.

Inside the brain are billions of cells. These cells send messages to your body. The cells are joined by tiny pathways called nerves. They can travel very quickly around the body. Our senses—sight, hearing, touch, taste, smell—send signals to the brain to let it know what is going on in the outside world.

The parts of the brain have different jobs to do.

The cerebrum is the biggest part of the brain. It is at the front. It controls thoughts and movement. It has two parts—the right brain controls the left side of the body, while the left brain controls the right side of the body.

The cerebellum controls movement and balance. It is at the back and bottom. It allows us to ride a bike or play an instrument. The hippocampus stores memories. The amygdala controls feelings. The brain stem is in charge of automatic things, like breathing. It connects to the spinal cord.

The brain does not move, but it still needs lots of energy. Blood flows to the brain to keep it alive. The human brain is truly amazing.

© MR STEGGELS ADVANCED INSTRUCTION PTY LTD

31. The biggest part of the brain is called the

    A   cerebellum
    B   hippocampus
    C   cerebrum
    D   stem

32. The job of the senses is to

    A   control thoughts and movement
    B   send messages to the brain
    C   control the body
    D   keep the brain alive

33. The cerebrum and the cerebellum are similar

    A   in size
    B   in controlling movement
    C   because they have two parts
    D   as they both store memories

34. Which of the following is not one of our senses?

    A   smell
    B   hearing
    C   fingertips
    D   sight

35. The brain is like a super fast computer because it

    A   keeps working even when you are asleep
    B   is made up of billions of cells
    C   sends messages very quickly
    D   allows us to ride a bike or play an instrument

END OF TEST

Test 4

1. The letters in the word **smile** can be rearranged to make a word meaning

    A   a distance to travel
    B   citrus fruits
    C   slippery liquid
    D   all of the above

2. Rearrange the words below to make the best sentence

    to   use   phone   me   text   a   send   mobile   your

    If the first word is **use**, what is the last word?

    A   phone
    B   mobile
    C   text
    D   me

3. The saying **a chip on your shoulder** means

    A   something good that isn't recognised at first
    B   when someone gives you a gift, don't be ungrateful
    C   being upset at something that happened in the past
    D   you cannot change who you are

4. The sum of two numbers is 30. One number is double the other. The difference between them is

    A   20
    B   15
    C   10
    D   5

© MR STEGGELS ADVANCED INSTRUCTION PTY LTD

5. I have some 5 cent coins, 10 cent coins & 20 cent coins. How many different ways can I make a total of 25 cents using these coins?

   A   3
   B   4
   C   5
   D   6

6. Carol is the not the shortest. Veda is taller than Jill. Jill is not as tall as Mona. Who is the shortest?

   A   Mona
   B   Veda
   C   Jill
   D   Carol

7. I am five years younger than my brother. I will be twelve next year. How old is my brother now?

   A   16
   B   15
   C   13
   D   17

8. I built this brick wall in my garden. Each brick cost $3. Some had to be cut in half to make the pattern. How much did the bricks cost in total?

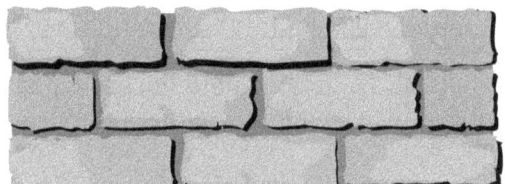

   A $ 25.00
   B $ 25.50
   C $ 26.50
   D $ 27.00

9. The word **turn** means the same as

   A   rotate
   B   move
   C   direction
   D   clockwise

Read the text and answer questions 10—14

The circus

Susan was very excited. It was her first time at the circus.

The tent was green with purple stripes. There were pretty, yellow lights all over it. It was held up by two huge metal poles that poked out of the top. Inside the tent was a large ring. There were two ladders facing each other. There was a thin, white rope between them. Beneath the rope was a black net. Susan asked her father what the rope and the net were for, and why there was a small pool beneath it. He told her to wait and see.

As the lights went down, a tiny red car came speeding into the ring. Susan wondered who could be driving. It was only big enough for a child. One of the doors suddenly flew open and out tumbled a clown. He ended up on his backside. Everyone laughed. He got up, dusted off his blue suit and shook his big, yellow hair. He didn't see the tiny car speeding up behind him. The audience screamed and pointed to warn him. At the last minute, he jumped out of the way and landed in the pool. There was a huge splash! Everyone laughed.

The clown's big yellow hair was flat and wet. The tiny red car stopped and out stepped a second clown. He was wearing a pink wig and a yellow suit. He pointed at the wet clown. He laughed so hard he almost fell over. The first clown leapt out of the pool and began chasing him. He chased him up one of the ladders. All the way to the top. The second clown had no choice but to walk out onto the rope. The first clown quickly followed him. They both looked very unsteady. They were wobbling and waving their arms about. Then, to Susan's amazement, a third clown got out of the car! He began throwing balls at the first two clowns to knock them off the rope. They clung to each other. Then they fell. The audience gasped.

The second clown grabbed the rope on the way down. The first clown grabbed his legs. They were hanging from the rope. The first clown began to slip. He pulled off the second clown's pants. He had white underpants with purple love hearts. Everyone laughed.

Then the clowns dropped into the net below, jumped onto the ground and chased the third clown back into the tiny car. It sped out of control and disappeared from the ring. Susan couldn't wait to see what happened next!

© MR STEGGELS ADVANCED INSTRUCTION PTY LTD

10. Susan was excited because

    A   the clowns fell off the high rope
    B   a tiny car red car came speeding into the ring
    C   she had never been to a circus before
    D   she couldn't wait to see what was next

11. What happened first?

    A   The third clown began throwing balls at the first two clowns
    B   The first clown chased the second clown up the ladder
    C   The clowns were wobbling and waving their arms about
    D   The car disappeared from the ring

12. When the clowns fell from the high rope, they landed

    A   in the car
    B   in the pool
    C   in the net
    D   on their backsides

13. Which clown was wearing a pink wig and a yellow suit?

    A   the first clown
    B   the second clown
    C   the third clown
    D   none of the above

14. Which word means **very surprised**?

    A   excited
    B   gasped
    C   amazed
    D   laughed

© MR STEGGELS ADVANCED INSTRUCTION PTY LTD

15. Which code should replace the question mark?

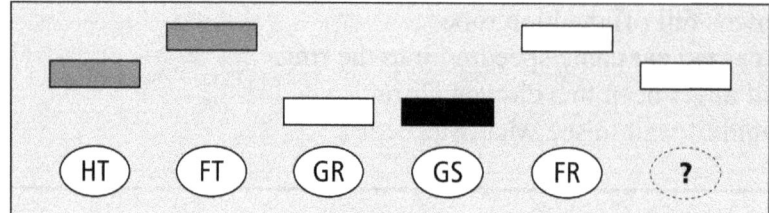

- A HT
- B FS
- C GT
- D HR

16. Fifty-one marbles were shared equally among 4 friends. How many marbles could not be shared?

- A 1
- B 2
- C 3
- D 4

17. You would find a **sparrow** in

- A the ocean
- B a supermarket
- C a garden shed
- D a tree

18. Which letters are missing?

BF, FJ, JN, __

- A NS
- B NR
- C MQ
- D NQ

19. Which word is the most opposite in meaning to **nervous**?

- A relaxed
- B scared
- C sleepy
- D worried

This bus timetable is for questions 20—21

Maxville	8:14	8:27
West Hills	8:18	8:31
Point Bon	8:23	8:36
Midvale	8:29	8:42
Oldtown	8:37	8:50
Central	8:43	8:56

20. I caught the bus at West Hills and got off at Central. How long was my trip?

    A   15 minutes
    B   23 minutes
    C   25 minutes
    D   35 minutes

21. I arrived at Oldtown at 8:39. How long do I have to wait for the next bus?

    A   2 minutes
    B   13 minutes
    C   12 minutes
    D   11 minutes

22. I started at this sign and rode to the Creek for a swim. Then I rode to the Kiosk for a drink. How far did I ride?

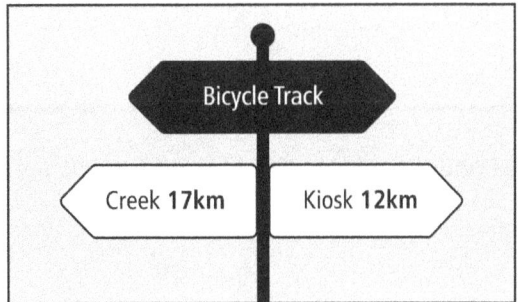

    A   17 km
    B   25 km
    C   46 km
    D   58 km

© MR STEGGELS ADVANCED INSTRUCTION PTY LTD

23. Two of these 3-letter groups can be joined to form a new word meaning **firm, solid, well built**.

    sec   ble   ats   lid   sta   ing   lev

   This new word begins with the letter

   A   l
   B   b
   C   s
   D   a

24. Describe this pattern from **left to right**

   A   Rotate the shape a quarter turn right
   B   Rotate the shape half a turn right
   C   Flip the shape to the left
   D   Flip the shape to the right

25. I am more than 30 but less than 60. I am an odd number. There is a 4 in my number. How many different numbers could I be?

   A   4
   B   5
   C   10
   D   11

26. If the code for **has** is **3k4** and the code for **wed** is **p92**, what will the code be for **washed**?

   A   pk4392
   B   pk4329
   C   p4k392
   D   pk2943

© MR STEGGELS ADVANCED INSTRUCTION PTY LTD

27. Unscramble these letters and choose which one of them is **something you could eat**

    A   ria
    B   uoseh
    C   cansk
    D   odow

28. Which is the odd one out?

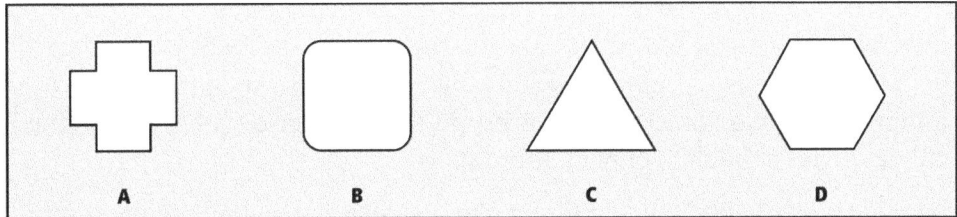

29. Which letter is next in the pattern?

                        Z, X, V, T, __

    A   R
    B   Q
    C   S
    D   P

30. Which shape completes the second pair in the same way as the first?

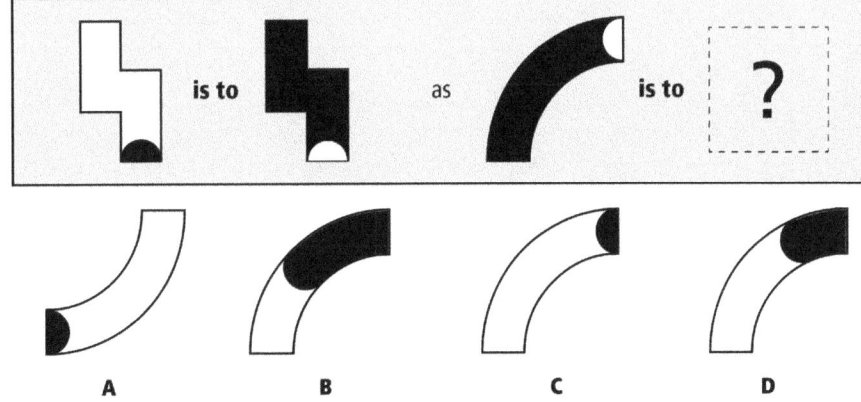

Read the text and answer questions 31—35

All children should have to play sport

Children do not play enough sport. Too much time is spent sitting still. It is unhealthy. All children need to move more. Playing sport is the best way to get kids moving.

Many kids these days are fat. They eat too much junk food, including chips, chocolate, ice cream and sweets. Soft drinks, like cola and lemonade are the biggest problem. They have lots and lots of sugar. So does fruit juice. Kids should be drinking more water. They should be playing more sport so they don't get fat.

Kids spend hours playing games on computers and tablets. They also spend too much time watching TV. Some kids sit for a long time doing homework. Kids need lots of exercise each day. It is not healthy for them to be sitting all day. Kids should be playing more sport.

Sport is fun. There are a lot of sports that kids can play. Soccer and netball are great sports to play in winter. Cricket and surfing are perfect for summer. Games that are played inside, like basketball, can be played all year round. Kids should be playing these sports.

Sport is a great way to meet new friends. Kids can learn to work together as a team. **This** teaches them new skills. It is better than being bored at home. Kids should be playing sport.

Children spend too much time sitting still. They need to play more sport. It is healthy. Kids can keep fit, have fun and make new friends. All children should have to play sport.

© MR STEGGELS ADVANCED INSTRUCTION PTY LTD

31. This text can best be described as

    A   an advertisement
    B   an argument
    C   a report
    D   a diary

32. According to the author, all children should have to play sport because

    A   they spend too much time playing games on computers and tablets
    B   it is a great way to meet new friends
    C   many kids these days are fat
    D   all of the above

33. The author

    A   repeats the same idea at the end of each paragraph
    B   does not have an opinion about sport
    C   has written in the past tense
    D   gives three reasons why kids should have to play sport

34. The word **this** in paragraph 5 refers to

    A   meeting new friends
    B   sport
    C   working together as a team
    D   new skills

35. Which is a fact, not an opinion?

    A   Playing sport is the best way to get kids moving
    B   There are a lot of sports that kids can play
    C   Soccer and netball are great sports to play in winter
    D   Kids spend too much time playing games on computers and tablets

© MR STEGGELS ADVANCED INSTRUCTION PTY LTD

END OF TEST

Test 5

1. Which pattern completes the second pair in the same way as the first?

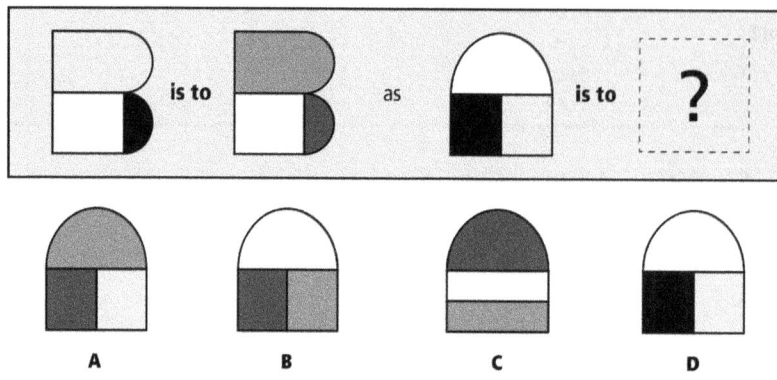

2. In a foreign language, **szu bje** means he was and **bje tuz** means she was. What is the foreign word for **she**?

   A   szu
   B   bje
   C   tuz
   D   she

This chart is for questions 3—4

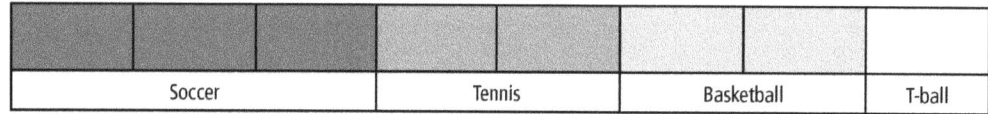

3. This bar chart shows sports chosen by students at my school. If 45 people chose soccer altogether, how many people chose T-ball?

   A   8
   B   15
   C   25
   D   30

4. How many students were included in the chart?

   A   40
   B   80
   C   120
   D   360

© MR STEGGELS ADVANCED INSTRUCTION PTY LTD

5. I can run 400m in one minute. How long will it take me to run 100m at the same pace?

   A   40 seconds
   B   25 seconds
   C   15 seconds
   D   10 seconds

6. The letters in **races** can be rearranged to form a new word meaning

   A   to dislike
   B   a type of fish
   C   a mark
   D   to frighten

7. Which pair of words is most similar in meaning?

   A   beat   lose
   B   come   before
   C   real   lie
   D   laugh   chuckle

8. **Frame** is to **window** as **motor** is to

   A   motorway
   B   bicycle
   C   car
   D   petrol

9. If A = 2, B = 4 and C = B + 3, then A + B + C =

   A   24
   B   13
   C   12
   D   none of the above

© MR STEGGELS ADVANCED INSTRUCTION PTY LTD

10. Someone who is **eager**

    A wants to do something very much
    B has the ability to do something
    C is very tired
    D is very responsible

11. I bought one book and one bookmark. Together they cost $12. The book cost $6 more than the bookmark. How much did I pay for the book?

    A $ 3
    B $ 6
    C $ 9
    D $ 10

12. Which is the odd one out?

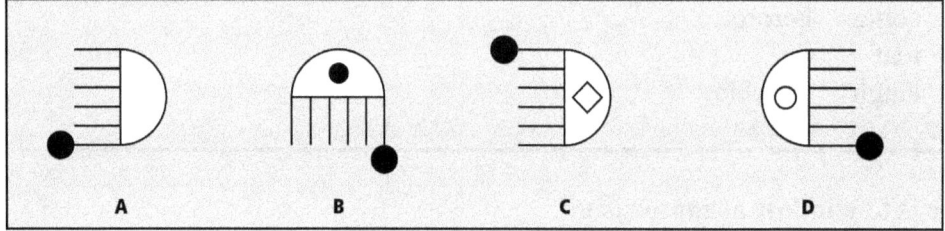

13. When I get out of bed, I take 10 minutes to get dressed, 15 minutes to eat breakfast and 15 minutes to walk to school. I need to be at band practice at 8:30 am. What time should I get out of bed?

    A 7:30 am
    B 7:40 am
    C 7:50 am
    D 8:00 am

14. These words all have something in common. Which word also belongs in this group?

    sardine   crab   whiting   shark

    A ray
    B cougar
    C eaglet
    D praying mantid

© MR STEGGELS ADVANCED INSTRUCTION PTY LTD

15. **Clown** is to **circus** as _____ is to _____

    A   waiter   waitress
    B   pop   music
    C   freezer   cold
    D   nurse   hospital

16. Which is next in the series?

    @@@@@   @@@@   @@@   @@
    $$$$$ $$$$$ $$$$$ $$$$$?
    %   %%   %%%   %%%%

    @@   @   @   @@@
    $$$$$ $$$$$ $$$$ $$$$$
    %%%%   %%%%%%   %%%%%%   %%%%%
    A   B   C   D

17. How many different ways are there to get from point A to point S moving only up and to the right?

    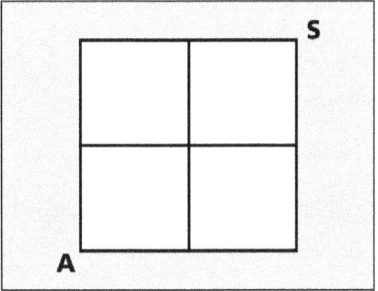

    A   2
    B   4
    C   6
    D   12

18. Complete the following saying

    If you can't stand the heat, get out of the _____.

    A   sun
    B   fire
    C   kitchen
    D   room

Read the text and answer questions 19—23

Teachers are witches!

Your teachers all are witches
They fly to school on brooms
When you're fast asleep in bed
They come out of their tombs

They soar above the clouds
And cackle as they fly
It makes them very happy
To hear their students cry

Their lessons are so awful
They tie your brains in knots
And if you do not understand
They boil you up in pots

They cover up their faces
Their bumpy warts and boils
Underneath the make-up
They look a lot like gargoyles

They gather in the staffroom
To bite the heads off rats
They use the tails for toothpicks
Then feed them to their cats

Dear reader please beware,
Those beasts you call your teachers
Even though they seem quite nice
Are very scary creatures!

© MR STEGGELS ADVANCED INSTRUCTION PTY LTD

19. The reader that the poet has in mind is

   A   a school student
   B   a teacher
   C   one of the witches
   D   an adult

20. This poet is trying to _____ the reader

   A   scare
   B   excite
   C   boil
   D   warn

21. Children don't know that their teachers are witches because they

   A   seem quite nice
   B   use make-up to cover their ugly faces
   C   arrive at school in the darkness
   D   all of the above

22. Which word means to be **alert to danger**?

   A   scary
   B   beware
   C   dear
   D   creatures

23. We can conclude that **gargoyles** must be

   A   witches
   B   teachers
   C   beautiful
   D   ugly creatures

© MR STEGGELS ADVANCED INSTRUCTION PTY LTD

24. Which figure completes the pattern?

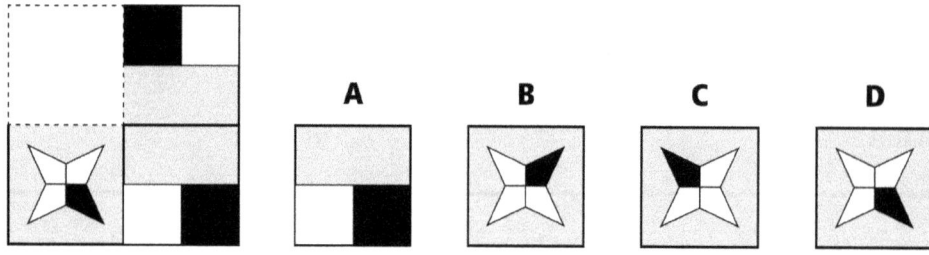

This chart is for questions 25—26

Student	Test 1	Test 2	Test 3	Test 4
Abe	15	13	16	14
Benedict	16	15	15	14
Carol	14	16	15	13
Diana	13	15	15	14
Edgar	17	13	14	15

25. Which student scored the highest total marks for all four tests?

    A   Abe
    B   Benedict
    C   Carol
    D   Edgar

26. Which is true?

    A   Carol had the lowest score
    B   Diana had the 2nd highest score
    C   Benedict scored below 60
    D   Two students had the same total score

27. What is the name given to **a group of ships?**

    A   armada
    B   clutter
    C   platoon
    D   squad

© MR STEGGELS ADVANCED INSTRUCTION PTY LTD

28. What is the time on this clock?

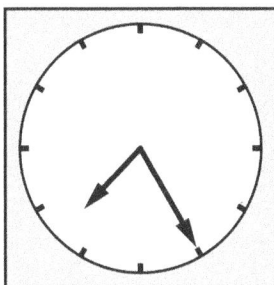

    A   8:25
    B   8:20
    C   7:25
    D   5:38

29. Which code should replace the question mark?

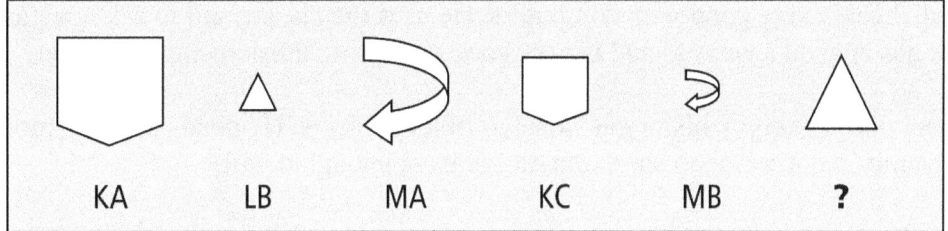

    A   LC
    B   LA
    C   MC
    D   KB

30. Which letter can be added to front of these letters to form words?

    __able   __hin   __ase   __heat

    A   s
    B   t
    C   b
    D   c

© MR STEGGELS ADVANCED INSTRUCTION PTY LTD

Read the text and answer questions 31—35

Glenview Public School—semester two

Student   Michael Chen
Teacher   Mr Simpson

English: Micheal has improved in reading. He is now on Grey level. His story writing is good but he needs to work on sentence structure and punctuation. He is happy to speak in front of the class.

Mathematics: Michael works on each topic well. He knows how to add, subtract, divide and multiply. He needs to work on problem solving as he sometimes finds it hard to understand the question.

Science: This is Micheal's favourite subject. He is very good at doing experiments in class. He understands why the sky is blue and what makes a rainbow. He organises his science reports well.

Technology: Michael is very good with computers. He uses the class email to ask questions and to help his classmates. He has created a website and is very good at making music using Hitmaker.

History: Michael does not enjoy history as much as other subjects. He needs to make more effort to research. His history reports are too short and do not have enough detail.

Geography: Micheal's project on Antarctica was very good. He was very interested in this topic. He even made a video for his project. Well done.

Art: Michael worked well at times in painting and drawing. He finds it hard to get ideas for his work. He likes to work with a partner. He behaved very well during the excursion to the art gallery.

Music: Michael is very good at music. He plays flute in the school band so he knows a lot about reading music. He also enjoys helping others to learn instruments.

Sport: Michael enjoys team games such as soccer and basketball. He works will with his classmates and plays fairly. He needs to work harder in gymnastics.

Overall, Michael performed well this term. Keep up the good work.

Mr Simpson

© MR STEGGELS ADVANCED INSTRUCTION PTY LTD

31. The main purpose of this text is to

   A   entertain
   B   explain
   C   argue
   D   inform

32. In which subject does Michael find it hard to understand the question?

   A   English
   B   mathematics
   C   technology
   D   history

33. In which subject does Michael like to work with another person?

   A   science
   B   technology
   C   art
   D   music

34. We can conclude that Michael

   A   is an outstanding student
   B   does very well in subjects he likes
   C   is not a very confident student
   D   enjoys gymnastics more than team sports

35. Which phrase can best replace **overall**?

   A   Taking everything into account
   B   All in all
   C   Taken as a whole
   D   all of the above

© MR STEGGELS ADVANCED INSTRUCTION PTY LTD

END OF TEST

Test 1 solutions

Q	A	Explanation
1	B	Kids' Menu is written at the top of the text
2	A	The main purpose of a menu is to tell the reader what is available at a restaurant
3	D	All of the above
4	C	The soft drinks listed on the menu are lemonade, cola, orange, creaming soda, passion fruit
5	C	beef burger $12 + Frozen ice cola $2.50 + Banana split $8.00 = $22.50
6	C	Skip two letters: A b c D e f G h I J k l M
7	D	Total number of mL = 120 + 220 = 340ml. Each jug needs 340 ÷ 2 = 170ml 120 + 50 = 170ml 220 – 50 = 170ml
8	C	bet = 432 tim = 251 bit = 452 emit = 3152
9	C	25 – 12 = 13 13 + 9 + 1 (teacher) = 23
10	C	A illustrator draws pictures for books etc
11	C	The asterisk is on the corner of the shape; not the edge as it is in A, B and D.
12	D	A B and C are all units of length. D millilitre is a measure of capacity.
13	B	36 ÷ 3 = 12 which is the middle number 11 + 12 + 13 = 36
14	B	3 bananas = 1 rock melon 9 bananas = 3 rock melon = 1 watermelon
15	D	someone something sometimes somehow
16	C	The writer was bored at school (it seemed to drag on forever) and now it looks like he'll be stuck inside all day.
17	B	The council has closed the ground because it is flooded. A, C and D are all opinions (likes and dislikes)
18	D	Mum and Dad will agree with the writer's little brother if there is a problem because he is youngest and the writer should be looking after him
19	D	Some people like being inside when it's raining… Not me. I like being outside. In any weather
20	D	A The rain is beating like a drum, no drum is actually being played. B It has been raining all week, not all weekend. C The author wants to be outside playing soccer.
21	C	deckhand: works on a ship shearer: removes the wool from sheep carpenter: works with wood woodsman: chops down trees
22	D	Top number in table x itself = bottom number 11 x 11 = 121
23	C	The possible number combinations are: (1,1 1,2 1,3 1,4 1,5 1,6) (2,2 2,3 2,4 2,5 2,6) (3,3 3,4 3,5 3,6) (4,4 4,5 4,6) (5,5 5,6) (6,6) (6 + 5 + 4 + 3 + 2 + 1 = 21)
24	C	A hornet, a locust and a fly are all insects. A husky is a dog.

25	A	6 small squares + 2 (4 x 4) squares left and right
26	B	A melon is a fruit. Parsley is a herb.
27	C	2.98 + (6 + 7) = 2.98 + 13 2.98 + 13 = 3.11
28	B	They saw the bus approaching their stop.
29	D	a = 5, n = 3. s = 8. w = 1, e = 9, r = 7
30	C	Before 7am = 5, 7am-8am = 30, 8am – 9am = 75 75 + 30 + 5 = 110
31	D	A = brown B = gold C = orange D = paper
32	D	The pattern: add one line each time. The pattern needs four lines.
33	A	One pair of shorts costs $12 (the difference between $32 and $20). One shirt costs $20 - $8 = $12
34	B	The tile is rotated 180 degrees
35	C	Reverse alphabet code: | A | B | C | D | E | F | G | H | I | J | K | L | M | N | O | P | Q | R | S | T | U | V | W | X | Y | Z | | z | y | x | w | v | u | t | s | r | q | p | o | n | m | l | k | j | i | h | g | f | e | d | c | b | a |

Test One score summary															
General ability	Question	6	8	10	11	12	15	21	24	26	28	29	31	32	34	35	Total
	Tick/cross																
Reading	Question	1	2	3	4	5	16	17	18	19	20	Total
	Tick/cross											
Mathematics	Question	7	9	13	14	22	23	25	27	30	33	Total
	Tick/cross											

Test 2 solutions

Q	A	Explanation
1	C	The writer mentions a raincoat, but not an umbrella.
2	B	1st → Water was coming in faster than I could spoon it out 2nd → lightning started 3rd → I saw a huge wave coming toward me 4th → I woke up
3	C	The thunder sounded like an angry giant roaring above the clouds.
4	D	giant, huge & enormous are synonyms—they all mean very large is size.
5	C	This text is a story or narrative. A = information text, B = explanation text, C = story, D = story. Since the story is not about having a bath, C is the best answer.
6	B	flour, sugar and eggs are all food items used in recipes. They are ingredients.
7	A	A daisy is a type of flower. A drill is a type of tool.

8	B	A dog is man's best friend. A dog is more loyal to its owner than any human friend will ever be.
9	C	The numbers are 9 and 18. 9 x 2 = 18 18 + 9 = 27 18 – 9 = 9
10	D	Betty > Joan > Milly youngest to oldest: Milly, Joan, Betty.
11	C	There are only three full weeks (Sunday to Monday) in this month; not four.
12	B	November has 30 days January, July and October have 31 days.
13	C	Every driver must follow the road rules.
14	C	pattern: x 3 – 5 6 x 3 = 18 18 – 5 = 13
15	B	danger means likely to case harm or injury safety means being protected from harm.
16	C	36 x 2 = 472 6 x 12 = 72
17	C	soap is used to clean a desk is used for writing.
18	C	This shape is 3 black blocks wide and 5 black blocks high. There are 15 blocks altogether. 15 x 2 = 30
19	C	From this signpost, Sandy beach is 5km away and Shark bay is 12km away. This means that they are 12 + 5 km away = 17 km away from each other.
20	C	The shape in the top left corner is being rotated ¼ turn to the right as it moves to the top right, then down to the bottom right, then across to the bottom left.
21	C	Take the first two letters of the 1st word and the second two letters of the 2nd word. seat + chat = seat
22	C	Seaside: by the sea Sideline: the line on each side of a court or playing field
23	B	X = large-sized shape Q = white Y = medium-sized shape R = grey Z = small-sized shape S = black
24	D	Top row: 5, 4, 9 2nd row: 10, 6, 2 3rd row: 3, 8, 7
25	C	The circle must be on the right side of the shape. The black right-angled triangle must be in the bottom left corner. The black and grey equilateral triangles top and bottom remain in the same place.
26	D	Entire means no part left out, whole, complete.
27	A	These are all capital cities of Australia. Brisbane is the capital of Queensland.
28	C	Antler is an anagram of learnt
29	C	Subtract 6 from the previous number 30 – 6 = 24
30	C	A son must have a mother. No one can be born without a mother.
31	D	The text tells the reader that they will need an adult helper, so it is for kids who want to cook.
32	C	The ingredients are also toppings (sliced onions, chopped capsicum, minced meat, sausage, pineapple chunks, sliced mushrooms, sliced olives and chopped herbs)
33	B	Spread tomato paste on base Arrange toppings Sprinkle on grated cheese Cook for 10 minutes

| 34 | D | Some ingredients need to be cut with a knife. An oven mitt is needed, so you don't burn yourself. There is a chance of getting cut or burnt. |
| 35 | A | Various toppings means to use a selection of or variety or those listed. |

Test Two score summary																
General ability	Question	6	7	8	13	15	17	20	21	22	23	26	27	28	29	30	Total
	Tick/cross																
Reading	Question	1	2	3	4	5	31	32	33	34	35	Total				
	Tick/cross															
Mathematics	Question	9	10	11	12	14	16	18	19	24	25	Total				
	Tick/cross															

Test 3 solutions

Q	A	Explanation
1	B	The Queen and King have to be at each end. If the Queen is to the left of the Ace, and the Jack is to the right, then only B is possible.
2	A	There are flowers in a garden. There are pages in a book.
3	C	The two words are caught (1) found and stopped a person trying to escape and court (2) an area drawn on the ground that is used for playing sport
4	B	c (%) a (#) t (@) e (!) r (>) r (>) e (!) a (#) c (%) t (@)
5	B	$ 1.50 + $ 2.30 = $ 3.80 $ 10.00 - $ 3.80 = $6.20
6	A	Handy: convenient to handle or use; useful. Expert: a person who is very knowledgeable about or skilful in a particular area. Neat: arranged in a tidy way; in good order. Useless: having no ability or skill in a specified activity or area.
7	C	There are two triangles and three rectangles in a triangular prism.
8	C	The pattern is + 6 then – 2 16 – 2 = 14
9	D	A car is a road vehicle with an engine, four wheels, and seats
10	B	Everyone in my family loves it, but I don't….something just doesn't feel right.
11	C	I get the feeling I have lived in this house before. But I couldn't have.
12	A	Even before we went into the house, I knew where everything was.
13	D	The lady who showed us the house didn't even know about the passageway.
14	B	The girl in the photograph was me! This is why the author had the feeling that she had lived in the house before.
15	C	2 apples = $4.10 1 apple = $2.05 3 apples = 3 x $2.05 = $6.15
16	D	Multiply X by 4 then subtract 1 to get Y. 3 x 4 = 12 12 – 1 = 11 9 x 4 = 36 36 – 1 = 35

#	Ans	Explanation
17	C	The shape has been rotated ¼ turn to the right. The black club and the white heart remain upright, but the lines change direction as they move with the shape.
18	C	A beverage is a drink other than water
19	A	Group A: moon Group B: light = moonlight
20	B	hem = 256 him = 236 mit = 634 t = 4 i = 3 m = 6 e = 5
21	D	gang: a number of people e.g. criminals gong: a metal disc that is hit to make a sound
22	C	Each kite shape that makes up 8 pointed star is half black and half white, so ½ of the entire star is shaded black.
23	B	Frank is 12. Ryan is half of 12 = 6. Ben is two years older than Ryan 6 + 2 = 8. Liam is one year older than Ben. 8 + 1 = 9
24	A	Pattern: skip 1 letter fwd: H i J E f G R s T O p Q F g H O p Q W x Y L m N
25	A	This is a symmetrical pattern; the column on the left is reflected on the right.
26	B	As thick as thieves refers to friends or people who have a very close bond and share private information
27	D	chance of spinning white = 2 out of 8 chance of spinning black = 1 out of 8 chance of spinning yellow= 3 out of 8 chance of spinning green = 2 out of 8
28	A	If Sunday was two days ago, today is Tuesday. Seven days from today will also be Tuesday, plus three more (to make 10) will be Friday.
29	D	A, B & C do not join to make a complete circuit, but D does.
30	C	In winter, the temperature is lower so people stay indoors.
31	C	The cerebrum is the biggest part of the brain. (paragraph 4)
32	B	Our senses—sight, hearing, touch, taste, smell—send signals to the brain to let it know what is going on in the outside world. (paragraph 2)
33	B	The cerebrum controls your thoughts and movement. (paragraph 4) The cerebellum controls movement and balance. (paragraph 5)
34	C	Our senses are: sight, hearing, touch, taste, smell. (paragraph 2)
35	C	Inside the brain are billions of cells. These cells send messages to your body. They can travel very quickly around the body. (paragraph 2)

Test Three score summary																
General ability	Question	2	3	4	6	9	17	18	19	20	21	24	25	26	29	30	Total
	Tick/cross																
Reading	Question	10	11	12	13	14	31	32	33	34	35	Total				
	Tick/cross															
Mathematics	Question	1	5	7	8	15	16	22	23	27	28	Total				
	Tick/cross															

Test 4 solutions

Q	A	Explanation
1	D	a distance to travel → miles citrus fruits → limes slippery liquid → slime
2	C	Use your mobile phone to send me a text.
3	C	The saying a chip on your shoulder means that you are angry or upset about something that happened in the past.
4	C	10 + 20 = 30 20 is double 10 20 – 10 = 10
5	B	5 + 5 + 5 + 5 + 5 = 25 5 + 5 + 5 + 10 = 25 5 + 10 + 10 = 25 5 + 20 = 25
6	C	tallest to shortest → Veda taller than Mona taller than Jill. Carol is not the shortest (she could be tallest, 2nd tallest or 3rd tallest)
7	A	I am 11 now (12 next year). My brother is 11 + 5 = 16
8	D	There are 8 full bricks and 2 half bricks in the wall. 8 + ½ + ½ = 9 $ 3 x 9 = $ 27
9	A	turn and rotate mean move in a circular direction
10	C	Susan was excited. It was her first time at the circus.
11	B	The first clown chased the second clown up the ladder The clowns were wobbling and waving their arms about The third clown began throwing balls at the first two clowns The car disappeared from the ring
12	C	Then the clowns dropped into the net below
13	B	…out stepped a second clown. This one was wearing a pink wig and a yellow suit
14	C	amazed: surprised (someone) greatly; filled with astonishment.
15	D	F = top position R = white G = bottom position S = black H = middle position T = grey
16	C	51 divided by 4 → 4 x 12 = 48 51 – 48 = 3
17	D	A sparrow is a small, plump, brown-grey bird with short tail and stubby beak
18	B	1st letter: B cde F ghi J klm N 2nd letter: F ghi J klm N opq R
19	A	Nervous means easily alarmed or worried. Relaxed means free from worry or stress.

20	C	West Hills 8:18 → Central 8:43 = 25 minutes
21	D	The next bus from Oldtown is at 8:50. 8:39 → 8:50 = 11 minutes
22	C	Starting at the sign, I rode 17 km to the Creek, then 17km back to the sign = 34 km Then I rode to the Kiosk → 34 km + 12 km = 46 km
23	C	sta + ble = stable = firm, solid, well built.
24	A	turn the shape a quarter turn to the right
25	B	all numbers with 4 between 30 and 60 → 34, 40, 41, 42, 43, 44, 45, 46, 47, 48, 49, 54 odd → 41, 43, 45, 47, 49
26	A	w = p a = k s = 4 h = 3 e = 9 d = 2 (pk4392)
27	C	A = air B = house C = snack D = wood
28	B	B has rounded corners. All other corners are sharp.
29	A	Pattern: skip 1 in reverse → Z y X w V u T s R
30	C	The shape remains in the same position, but black and white change. D does not have enough black shaded.
31	B	This text is an argument. It argues one side of an issue—that kids need to play more sport.
32	D	A: paragraph 3 B: paragraph 5 C: paragraph 2
33	A	repeated idea: Kids should be playing sport
34	C	This = working together in a team
35	B	A, C and D are opinions. B is a fact—there are many sports that kids can play

Test Four score summary															
General ability	Question	1	2	3	9	15	17	18	19	23	24	26	27	28	29	30	Total
	Tick/cross																
Reading	Question	10	11	12	13	14	31	32	33	34	35	Total
	Tick/cross											
Mathematics	Question	4	5	6	7	8	16	20	21	22	25	Total
	Tick/cross											

Test 5 solutions

Q	A	Explanation
1	B	White sections remain white. Black sections become dark grey. Dark grey sections become light grey.
2	C	bje is the only repeated foreign word, so it matches was. Then szu = he and tuz = she
3	B	soccer has 3 segments. 45 ÷ 3 = 15. Each segment in the chart = 15.
4	C	There are 8 segments altogether. Each segment is worth 15. 15 x 8 = 120
5	C	400m in 1 minute → 400m in 60 seconds. Divide both by 4 → 100m in 15 seconds.
6	D	races becomes scare which means to frighten
7	D	laugh and chuckle are synonyms
8	C	A frame is part of a window. A motor is part of a car.
9	B	2 + 4 + 7 = 13
10	A	eager means enthusiastic. Someone who is enthusiastic wants to do something very much.
11	C	If both items cost the same, they would be $6 each. One is $6 more than the other, so subtract $3 and add it to $6, then take the other $3 and subtract it from $6. $6 + $3 = $9 $6 - $3 = $3 ($9 - $3 = $6)
12	A	There is no small shape inside the white semi-circle
13	C	Time taken to get ready → 10 mins + 15 mins + 15 mins = 40 minutes. 8:30 am – 40 mins = 7:50 am
14	A	These are all sea creatures. A ray is a sea creature (e.g. sting ray). A cougar is a cat. An eaglet is a baby eagle bird. A praying mantid is an insect.
15	D	A clown works in a circus. A nurse works in a hospital.
16	B	Top line: @ decreases by one Middle line: $ remains the same Bottom Line: % increases by one
17	C	Without going backwards, there are 6 different ways:
18	C	If you can't stand the heat, get out of the kitchen means if you can't cope, you should leave the task to someone who can manage it.

19	A	The poet directly speaks to a school student. Your teachers, when you're fast asleep, tie your brains in knots if you do not understand.
20	D	Dear reader please beware → warning
21	D	They cover their faces with make-up, underneath they look like gargoyles—an ugly carved human or animal face or figure projecting from the gutter of a building, typically acting as a spout to carry water clear of a wall. Even though they seem quite nice When you're fast asleep in bed, they come out of their tombs.
22	B	Beware means to be cautious and alert to danger
23	D	Underneath the make-up, they look a lot like gargoyles. The witches cover their ugly faces so the children don't realise that they are witches.
24	C	The top row is reflected in the bottom row. The shapes are then reversed.
25	B	Abe: 58 Benedict: 60 Carol: 58 Diana: 57 Edgar: 59
26	D	Both Abe and Carol scored 58
27	A	armada of ships clutter of cats / spiders platoon of soldiers squad of soldiers / players
28	C	The long hand (minute hand) is pointing to the 5th dash from the top → 25 minutes The short hand (hour hand) is pointing in between the 7 and the 8, which means it is past 7 and not yet 8. 7:25
29	A	K = pocket shape A = large L = triangle B = small M = arrow C = medium
30	D	cable chin case cheat
31	D	A school report gives parents information about their child's learning. The purpose is to inform.
32	B	Mathematics: Michael works on each topic well. He knows how to add, subtract, divide and multiply. He needs to work on problem solving. Sometimes he finds it hard to understand the question.
33	C	Art: Michael worked well in painting and drawing this term. He finds it hard to get ideas for his work. He likes to work with a partner.
34	B	A: Michael is not good in every subject so he is not outstanding B: Michael likes computers, science, music and sport, but not history or art C: Michael is happy to speak in front of the class so he is confident D: Michael enjoys teams games but needs to work harder on gymnastics
35	D	Overall means Taking everything into account, All in all and Taken as a whole

Test Five score summary															
General ability	Question	1	2	6	7	8	10	12	14	15	16	18	24	27	29	30	Total
	Tick/cross																
Reading	Question	19	20	21	22	23	31	32	33	34	35	Total				
	Tick/cross															
Mathematics	Question	3	4	5	9	11	13	17	25	26	28	Total				
	Tick/cross															

www.ingramcontent.com/pod-product-compliance
Lightning Source LLC
LaVergne TN
LVHW061316060426
835507LV00019B/2183

9780648096719